A LIFE OF
Freedom

BREAKING THE STRONGHOLD
OF MENTAL ILLNESS

HOPE CAMPBELL

Book Cover Design: Prize Publishing House

Printed by Prize Publishing House, LLC in the United States of America.

First printing edition 2023.

Prize Publishing House

P.O. Box 9856, Chesapeake, VA 23321

www.PrizePublishingHouse.com

Library of Congress Control Number: 2023918563

ISBN (Paperback): 979-8-9892479-0-5

ISBN (E-Book): 979-8-9892479-1-2

Table of Contents

Introduction

In my life's most difficult, darkest time, all I had to turn to was God. I was broken, abused, confused, rejected, neglected, and abandoned. God was my safe place when I had no one to talk to. God was my peace when I was confused and broken. God saw the best in me even when I did not see it in myself. God was my comfort when I needed to cry. God was my confidence when I lost all hope.

I suffered silently from mental illness for five years of my life. I had a disease many people suffer from today that goes unnoticed. Suffering silently from mental illness for five years, I learned how to mask the pain within. No one knew that I heard voices. No one knew I was suicidal. No one knew I was depressed and oppressed.

I was mentally bound and confused, trying to find my way in this dark world of deception. I was isolated from reality because of the hidden trauma that suppressed half of my life. For years, I masked the pain by hurting others just to feel the comfort and void I was dealing with.

So many times in life, we are taught to be tough and hide how we feel and what we are dealing with emotionally and mentally. The first step to a healthy recovery is admitting you are broken and need help.

So many people hide their sickness because of fear of being labeled, hospitalized, rejected, and so much more. Understanding the root cause of mental illness is the key to a healthy healing process. I was healed from mental illness without doctors and without medication. It was all God.

When I first realized that something within me was different, I could not hide how I felt or how unique my gifts and talents were around other people. I would see myself in a new light, shining brighter than others. I would see things before they happened. I would tell people things that I knew nothing about. I was setting people free even when I was in the world of sin.

Even while having sex, drinking, doing drugs, pimping women, running with kingpin dope dealers, and hanging with doctors, lawyers, members of Congress, senators, governors, and CEOs of major companies (all who were living a double life of getting high while working and turning up after parties of winning major deals) a part of me was convicted not understanding that my spiritual connection to God was the reason I felt so guilty and wanted to stop living a life of sin.

I had no idea at the time that I was God's chosen prophet. I did not understand the unique gifts I had. All I knew was the fast life of the streets. What's so amazing about God is that He would send people to me out of nowhere to tell me about who God said I would be and the things I would do throughout the earth. At that time, I thought, *what could God possibly do with my life?*

I am in these streets doing everything sinful and not pleasing before God. I was a hot mess, though, I thought. I felt like there was no hope for me, and I know some of you who will read this book feel the same way as I once did at some point in your life. After years of running the streets, I was finally tired and ready for a change.

I will never forget hanging out with my friends one night and sitting there getting high to the point I was numb to everything happening around me. I told all my friends I was done doing drugs and with this lifestyle. God has more for me than this. I am going to be traveling the world and working for God.

I will be a wealthy woman with many businesses for the kingdom. They all laughed at me and thought I was losing my mind, but little did they know I was done with everything that night.

I got up, ran out the door to my mom's house, and cried and cried to God while in the shower. I vowed to God that I would never go back if He set me free from this lifestyle that was causing me nothing but pain. And just like that, it was over. The drugs, the alcohol, the sex, everything was over. I did not have a desire for any of it. I did not have withdrawals from wanting drugs. No rehab. No doctors. It was all God.

After years of surrendering, I still tried to find my way through life. I spent more time working on myself while pursuing my nursing career. I had finally found my passion and was good at my job. I was learning a lot and staying busy, so I would not deal with the hidden trauma (sounds familiar?). I stayed busy so I would not have to deal with the issues that lay dormant. I had learned a new way to mask the pain and function fully without anyone knowing my addictions.

Just when I thought everything was over, I was introduced to a new way of hiding the trauma. Not understanding or acknowledging the vow to God, I forgot all about what I said as I was praying and crying out for help. All I was looking at was a new way to hide the pain and trauma within myself.

While working in the medical field, I was introduced to drugs in a whole new way. I could work 12 to 16 hours high on drugs and function like a pro. The doctor taught me how to function and maintain while working.

Now, my mind was blown away at the fact that this surgeon was working high off cocaine and great at his job. My mind was like, *yes, I can do it as well.* Teach me all I need to know so I can maintain my high and still get this money.

We would hang out after work all the time. That is how I was introduced to the lawyers, senators, governors, police officers, mayor, members of Congress, other doctors, CEOs of major companies, and many others. We hung out so much I was considered family. I learned a lot about how people in the world were being deceived by the ones that were deemed so trustworthy.

While working in the medical field, I began to hear all kinds of sounds and voices out of nowhere. I thought maybe I was overworked or too high, so I ignored it altogether. Not understanding my prophetic gift was getting stronger; God was showing me what was about to happen so suddenly with my life.

Throughout my career as a nurse, I continued to hear voices and still was getting high to cope with the voices I was hearing in my head. After five years of suffering silently, I knew I was dealing with a mental illness no one could help me with but God.

I had to learn that the problem I had was with myself. I could not blame others because of how I felt about myself. The people were the roots that grew from the seeds I planted from my thoughts and actions. My story of overcoming mental illness is to help you understand that you are not alone and there is hope and help to live a life of mental freedom.

I am here to share my journey of how God gave me unconditional love and peace while healing. I am here to share how God gave me strategies and the blueprints that set me free. While we embrace the journey together, there will be many times you cry. There will be times you feel sad, but you will continually feel God's presence healing you and restoring you while giving you unconditional love.

My prayer to each individual who reads this manual is that the power of God will forever change your life, and you will know that with God, all things are possible.

Blessings to you,

Hope

CHAPTER 1

A Renewed Mind, Body, And Spirit

Dig deep within to heal, activate, surrender, and most of all, let go of all the hurt so you can heal and walk into your divine God-ordained purpose.

Let's take a look at how it all began. It all started the very first time you experienced rejection and hurt by family.

As a child, you always wanted the love and affection from your mother or father.

Not understanding why your dad seemed like he really never had time for you put you in a mind of feeling rejected.

Not understanding why your mom constantly abused you because of how your father treated her left you feeling abandoned.

Growing up was not easy. Trying to figure out your identity and holding on to the thought of wanting to be accepted by others caused you to find other ways to find comfort and love.

As a child, the damage was done by family members who were close to you.

You were forced to grow up very early in life, causing you to miss out on being a child who wanted to be loved.

Over the years, you grew up feeling abandoned and rejected because of all the hurt you experienced as a child. Not understanding why things happened to you, you began to blame yourself for what happened to you.

It caused you to mask the pain you were feeling. You found ways to comfort the pain just for a quick fix and a lifetime of mind isolation and bondage.

Often, we suppress the trauma with what is convenient and familiar.

Let's look at the trending pattern of toxicity in your family, friends, and even relationships.

First, the verbal abuse destroyed your character, and then it became more and more over time, where you began to believe every word that was said about you.

Not looking at the pattern, you continued to seek love and comfort only to end up broken, feeling like giving up and feeling like you would never be free. The pain continued to grow within more and more; no one could hear or see the inner secrets and words running through your mind.

Lost in your identity, you could not see the abuse because of a toxic mindset of bondage, confusion, isolation, and torment.

Wrapped up in the illusion that everything was okay, you fed off of negative energy and wasted time on unhealthy fruit that would not grow because of dead roots.

When a tree has dead roots, nothing can produce, nothing can blossom, and nothing can be transformed. When a tree is dead, all the tree is good for is being chopped down, uprooted, and hauled off to be cut up for firewood.

Think about it the same way with your spirit. If you do not feed your spirit daily, you will be delusional, hearing every voice besides God's voice, wavering, gossiping, and causing confusion amongst others and yourself.

Not understanding the devices of the enemy feeds your spirit with discord and trauma because of depression and identity crisis.

When you are battling mentally in your mind, you have to allow God to feed your mind with the goodness of His love through prayer, allowing Him to heal your deep secret wombs.

You have to allow God to take total control of the hidden parts no one can see with the natural eye. Surrendering to God's will gives you an unexplainable peace. You cannot obtain it in the natural way of thinking.

Understand in order to truly walk in your God-ordained purpose, you have to be willing to dig up the wombs of your past and present.

It is not always an easy process to revisit the dark secrets of your past. Why? Because it is hurtful, it brings back the trauma, it brings the anger out all over again, it brings the rejection to your thought process, and it makes you not want to confront the past because of suppressed emotions that you hid from everyone.

Once God opens your heart, you have to allow Him to give you a holy dose of sedation so the trauma will not cause permanent damage.

The sedation gives a sense of ease so you can face the dark secrets to be healed. With that sedation, it will wear off with ease so you can release the pain and cry out to God with a mind of freedom, knowing that the womb has had a surgery encounter with God.

Think about when performing surgery. You cannot have an operation until you are under sedation. Once the surgery is over, you are awakened by the nurse and still heavily sedated. Once the sedation wears off, you are coming into a feeling of the natural pain from the surgery.

The same applies to spiritual surgery. Once you are sedated with the holy dose of God's spirit, you are now able to open up the heart so the pain can surface. Once the heart is open, God can perform surgery gently.

After the recovery stage, you can now open up with fewer scars and pain to confront the trauma that causes you to feel defeated and abandoned.

Understand when God gives you ways to be free, you cannot take a detour or another route because of the feeling of being uncomfortable. Being uncomfortable is the process of healing because the pain has been hidden and not dealt with for years because of suppression.

When you have years of trauma that have been buried, you will feel discomfort, anger, emotions, sadness, and anxiety all at the same time, and the only thing that will give you freedom is God's love and allowing Him to uproot the broken you.

Being broken and vulnerable sometimes will allow you to end up in a toxic, unhealthy relationship that will leave you depressed, angry, hurt, confused, and still seeking love with a toxic mindset.

As you follow these steps to healing and breakthrough, take a break from social media. The only things you need to post are inspirational things or things from the Bible when God leads you to post.

This will feed your spirit with spiritual food. There is too much toxic behavior that is being displayed because of rejection and anger. Take time out and get to know yourself deeper and get to know your children in a new way.

These are the scriptures to meditate on daily.

- Isaiah 55:6
- Psalm 141:1-5
- Philippians 4:6
- Psalms 86:1-7
- Colossians 4:1-6

Every day, I want you to confess this over your life.

- I am healed.
- I am an overcomer.
- I am a product of excellence.
- I am chosen.
- I am the head and not the tail.

- I am a new creature in Christ Jesus.

- I have a purpose of living a great life.

- I am a wife. Proverbs 31 is my portion.

- I am honored by my husband.

- I am loved by God.

- I am a strong man of God.

- I have the power to create a great foundation for my family.

- I will stand tall as the husband/father of my household.

- I am a man of great value.

- I have the DNA of my Father, God.

- I am a man of wisdom. I am a man with a mind of Christ Jesus.

Confess this over and over, and you will see God move in your life in a mighty way.

Letting go often means letting go of family and friends.

Everyone cannot go where you are going.

Everyone cannot see the purpose in your life.

Everyone cannot see the greatness within you.

When you allow God to change your life, everything about you changes for the better. Stop fighting a spiritual battle with fleshly words. You will lose the battle every time.

When the devil fights you, you have to fight him in the spirit with prayer, fasting, and God's word. Learn your weapons!!!

Let's go a little deeper. I want you to think back on the very first time you felt vulnerable, rejected, or abandoned.

How did it make you feel?

When you answer this question, it is going to take you to a place that has been blocked for years.

You have to let go of the trauma and embrace the new you. Allowing God to heal you is essential to your health and well-being.

Think back to the very first time someone lied to you. Think about how it made you feel. You became angry and distant because of the lies, and it became a pattern that you were accustomed to after a while.

Throughout life, you are given choices. It is up to you what you will allow and what you will not allow.

Think back to the very first time you cheated on someone or someone cheated on you.

How did you make that person feel?

How did you feel when you found out that they were cheating?

Did you accept the cheating just for love?

Did you make excuses for their behavior?

If your answer is yes to any of these questions, you accepted the behavior of abuse because of low self-esteem and insecurities about who you are as a woman/man.

As you go deeper, God is going to uproot all the hurt that has caused you trauma over the years.

Ask yourself these questions and be totally honest and real with yourself.

- What causes the trauma in your mind?
- Why are you angry?
- What is it within yourself that you do not like, and you hide it?
- Why do you feel rejected?
- Why do you feel abandoned?
- What do you like about yourself?
- Do you really love yourself? Do not answer until you have examined everything within.
- Why do you like toxic relationships?

Understand you attract what you are. If you are broken, you will attract the same. If you are dealing with rejection, you attract the same. If you are dealing with brokenness, you attract the same, etc.

I want you to keep a journal of everything you experience during this time of transformation. Talk to God in your writing. Express your feelings through writing. Let go of emotions through your writing.

As you begin surgery, allow yourself time to heal. No excessive phone calls, no excessive social media. This is the time for you to hear God's voice with clarity and understanding. This is the time for you to love yourself and allow God to love you unconditionally.

Say this prayer daily.

Heavenly Father, I come before You seeking help and guidance. I need You to give me direction for my life, my purpose, and my destiny.

God, I ask You to take over my life. I need You to guide me in all truth. I thank You, Jesus, for clarity and understanding on how to be a great wife. I thank You, Jesus, for Your direction on how to be a great mother.

God, I thank You for giving me an understanding of how to be a great father and husband. God, guide me on how to love my wife.

God, guide me on how to love my children and teach them the right way. God, I invite You into my space, and I ask You to take over my life.

Thank You, Jesus, in advance for my identity in Christ Jesus. God, I thank You that every soul tie is broken off my life in Jesus' name.

I thank You.

I am free from all types of abuse.

I am free from all spirit husbands that have hindered me from receiving my husband in the natural way.

God, I thank You that all spirit wives have broken off my life. God, I thank You for a mind of freedom.

I thank Jesus for the eyes to see in the spirit. Thank You, Jesus, for a spirit of discernment. Thank You, Jesus, for wisdom, for I am married to wisdom.

I give You all of me. God, use me for Your glory. Thank You in advance, God, for deliverance and breakthrough.

I decree and declare I will see the reward of the wicked. I decree and declare I am victorious in Christ Jesus. God, thank You.

Today is a new day in my life, and I will walk boldly in my authority in Jesus' name. Amen.

As you go throughout your day, read this over and over again.

CHAPTER 2

Letting Go Of The Pain

- Write down what you want.

- How do you truly feel about yourself? (be honest)

- What are your thoughts about yourself?

- What do you see when you look in the mirror?

Once you have identified how you feel about yourself, ask yourself this question: Why?

Why do you feel this way?

As you read it out loud, begin to let go mentally. Once you begin to speak about it, the more you will feel a release to go further to experience freedom. Understand that when you have spent years of being traumatized, all you know is rejection and hurt. You become accustomed to the behavior of anger. Anger is a behavior displayed in many ways, such as manipulation. You will manipulate a person because of revenge. It manifests in control, wanting everything to go your way. It will manifest in pride, pretending you have it all together, and you will lie to keep up the false pretense of the real you.

Now that you have identified how you feel about yourself, it is time to ask yourself this question: What made you feel this way?

Asking yourself this question will open you up to the real truth of what caused the trauma, how you suppressed it for so many years, and how you found different ways to cope with the anger and isolation. Isolating yourself from people is when you are tormented the most. When learning how to deal with your anger and hurt, you will become depressed, not understanding how to deal with the pain. You will become mentally isolated, developing a pattern of mentally blocking out the trauma by suppressing it with drugs, alcohol, sex, manipulation, control, envy, and jealousy, just to name a few.

Digging deep within and going through the healing process will sometimes cause mixed emotions and feelings you never had to deal with. There will be thoughts running through your mind, feelings of being exposed, and feeling like God does not love you. Embracing the truth about yourself and the trauma you experienced is the first step to healing. You will begin to feel like God sent you help right when you thought all hope was lost. God loves you enough to send you help and wants you to live abundantly in peace, love, and joy.

Identifying the hurt will sometimes leave you feeling empty because of the impact of the trauma. So many people experience trauma so deep that they have put up a mental block and will not deal with the truth. People can't recall the trauma experienced throughout life when they have a mental block. Many people find ways to cope with the trauma they suffered so many years ago. Below are a few ways many cope with the trauma experienced.

- Self-medicating
- Prescription drugs
- Street drugs
- Alcohol
- Same-sex marriage/relationships
- Multiple sex partners
- Lying
- Mental, physical, and emotional abuse
- Controlling behavior
- Manipulative behavior
- Overworking oneself

Now that we have identified some ways people cope with trauma, how does this help you identify your coping method?

How do you cope with the hurt, trauma, and abuse you have suffered?

What gives you pleasure?

How do you feel when the excitement or high is over?

Do you feel depressed, angry, and confused?

Answering these questions will give you a clear view of how you have affected many people's lives and your own. The first important step to healing is admitting that you have a problem and need help.

Now that we have identified what helps you to cope with the trauma you have experienced over the years let's go deep into how we can manifest the inner you so you can fulfill your God-given purpose on earth.

*Father, I come to You asking You to forgive me of my sins and repent to God for (**call out your sins**). Father, I thank You for washing my mind in the blood of Jesus. Father, thank You for giving me a new mindset on how I see myself. Father, thank You for giving me my true identity in Christ Jesus. Give me an understanding of how to navigate the life I have been given.*

Father, thank You for restoration. Father, I thank You for the God-given purpose that You have given me. I decree and declare that my mind and thoughts are saturated in the blood of Jesus. I decree and declare that my mind is free from bondage. I take control of my thoughts and let go of the pain. I embrace my new identity in Christ Jesus. Today, I confess that my mind is free from my past, and I hold on to the promises of God.

CHAPTER 3

God's Love For You

Dealing with the real you requires removing the mask to see all the pain that has been hidden for years. Together, we walk through the steps of inner healing. Now, it is time to reflect and relive all the pain that has been buried.

1. Take off the title of being mom or dad.

2. Set your career to the side.

3. Let go of what the world has to say about you.

4. Embrace the pain that has caused you trauma (LET GO).

5. Forgive the person who hurt you.

6. Forgive yourself.

7. Take off the title of the church.

Letting go of everything that has held you bound for years gives you a peace you never experienced. Making a conscious decision to let go is not easy, nor is it fun to relive the hurt of your past. The most important thing about change and freedom is embracing the real you: the good, the bad, and the ugly.

Inner healing gives you a true insight into who you really are as an individual. You begin to learn different things about yourself that you never knew. So many times, we feel like no one understands what we go through. No one cares enough to help. Often, we feel like we are all alone. The truth is it is a spirit of confusion that is racing through our minds.

Now, it is time to deal with the real you.

- Look at yourself in the mirror and tell yourself, "I am important."

- Tell yourself, "I am worthy of love."

- Tell yourself, "I am worthy to be loved."

- Embrace the love God has for you.

- You are special to God.

- Tell yourself, "God loves me."

As you are being healed internally, it is important to love on yourself. Encouraging yourself will help you to see that there is a beautiful light at the end of the tunnel. Letting go of the pain is not a comfortable process, and I know you feel like you are torn between the two.

I know this is not what you planned for your life. You once had visions and dreams. I know you wanted to be a successful doctor, lawyer, hair stylist, etc. But life happened and caused you to take a detour off the path God designed for you. You must understand you do not always get what you want or choose for your life.

When you have a purpose and a calling, God will always redirect you. Redirection is not comfortable when you ignore the route intended in the beginning. Often, God will show us things, and we ignore them because of an unfamiliar path. We ignore them because we do not have enough clarity.

When we do not understand, we do things that feel good. We do things that are comfortable. We feed into the fleshly desires. We ignore the truth about who we really are because of the likes and familiarity of people.

Often, letting go means you lose friends and family. The most important thing to remember is when you begin to see life differently, some people will think you are acting funny or different. When experiencing mental freedom, you begin to see and feel different about life and yourself.

When you are mentally free, you are not consumed by your environment, but your environment will be consumed by the change they see within you. Here is a list of things to affirm you throughout your journey of freedom.

- I am not bound by my past.
- I am an overcomer.
- I am healed.
- I am restored.
- I am prepared for excellence.
- I am in control of my life.
- I am in love with me.

The more you confess these things, the more you will see and feel empowered to do great and mighty works. You will begin to feel compelled to do more and conquer more each day. When experiencing mental freedom, there is nothing you cannot accomplish. Holding on to the promises of God is vital to conquering the fear that plagues your mind daily. Allowing God access to construct your thoughts about life, who God chose you to be, and seeing it all manifest is a great accomplishment.

CHAPTER 4

Embracing The Path Of Freedom

Growing up being neglected and abused, you become accustomed to what you think is normal. Even when God puts people in your path to help you, you reject the help because of fear, fear of the unknown, and not trusting God to let go. God will always show us what is possible by letting go, but we ignore it because we do not want to.

Sometimes, you feel like what your life looks like now is good. You look at yourself like you are good; everyone around you can see the brokenness. When others can see what you hide, you act in your emotions because of pride. You lash out at the very one that God sent to help you.

Letting go, you have to face that you played a part in some of the things that happened. Realizing what happened in your life will give you peace to let go.

Allowing your mind to heal means being around positive people, speaking life to your situation daily, self-love and care, reading God's word, and most importantly, worship and prayer.

Why? Because it creates an atmosphere for God to dwell and commune with you daily.

Stop ignoring the help. Embrace the fact that you need help and consciously decide that you are worth the investment.

Understand when you are mentally intoxicated, you think you are not worthy of being mentally free because of what you allowed people to speak over your life. Life and death lie in the power of your tongue. You have the power to speak life or damnation. It should never get to the point that you allow someone to speak damnation or a curse over your life.

This is what you should say to yourself every day.

- I am the head, not the tail
- I am more than a conqueror.
- I am authorized to speak life.
- God has chosen me for a divine purpose.

Letting go means your circle will become really small, and many people will think you are acting differently because of the development of your mindset. They feel you are acting differently because you no longer think on a low level.

At this point, you have elevated how you think about yourself and your future. When experiencing mental freedom, you no longer think about what people think about you, nor do you wake up to please people.

Giving God a real YES means you no longer compromise for the likes of the enemy. You must make a conscious decision daily to change for the better. Spending time with God is the number one factor to freedom. Praying, fasting, and reading God's word are the ailments you need to succeed.

Making no compromising decisions means you will stand the test of time and fight for what is right. Giving God all of you means that God can now take control and elevate your life for the better.

You cannot allow people and their emotions to distract you when elevating. Being distracted will cause you to second-guess, doubt, fear, and compromise the purpose and calling on your life.

In life, we have a choice to live in chaos or peace. Living in peace, you focus more on being around positive and uplifting people. Being around people who can push you and cultivate your gift is essential to your next level.

The key to elevation is maintaining a posture for God to speak, impart, and transform your life. Understanding the mysteries of God requires you to live a lifestyle of holiness, which means fasting, praying, worshiping, and studying the word of God will become an everyday lifestyle.

Letting go, you must make a mental decision to embrace a new thought process on how you view life and let go of all past hurts to move forward. Mentally preparing your mind, you have to feed your thoughts on the things of God and not the things pleasing to your flesh.

When embracing a new life, you will see life differently and embrace the path God ordained for your life. Here are some confessions to help along this wonderful journey called freedom.

- My mind is free to embrace God's love.
- My mind is free from my past.
- My mind is wrapped in the blood of Jesus.
- God loves me. I am His daughter/son.

- The path God has for my life is great.

- Today, I confess God's wisdom empowers my mind.

- I am intelligent.

- I am smart.

- I will conquer the impossible.

- I am strong through God.

- God is my safe place.

As you confess this daily, you will see God move mightily in your life. You will see things happen out of nowhere because you allowed God to take over. God will teach you, guide you, and love you in the process of healing and restoration. It will be an incredible journey. You will be amazed at how God transforms your life for the world to see His goodness and faithfulness.

CHAPTER 5

Taking Off The Mask

Now, it is time to stop hiding behind a successful career. Now, it is time to stop deceiving your husband/wife. Some of you slept your way to the top. Some of you lied to get to the top. Some of you deceived others for success. Some of you manipulated your way to success.

You hide behind success because you are broken, confused, and hurt from your past that has held you bound for years. You hide the pain for years with the mask of having it all together and feel you do not need to express your feelings. You feel like you will be great as long as you have control. You feel you can control everything around you.

Being neglected, abused, molested, and angry gives you a sense of power mentally to hurt others before they hurt you. Wake up in the morning, look in the mirror, and give yourself a deceitful pep talk. Now, you have mentally prepared your mind to control and deceive the minds of the weak.

You have now put the mask on. Working two or three jobs, hiding behind college, lashing out in anger at anyone who begins to see the hurt, you find ways to make them feel like it is them with the issue and problem.

You begin to perform for the crowd that cares nothing about you. Now, you look like a clown in a circus. Why? Because the people you are performing for are talking about you behind your back.

There are guidelines and orders for healing. If you want to be healed, you must have an obedient spirit that will take rebuke and correction to grow.

Being humble and walking in humility does not mean you are weak or a punk. It means you are submitted to the will of God for your life, and it signifies that you need God in every area of your life for direction.

Being submissive to God gives you a new outlook on life and peace, knowing that God is leading and guiding you every step of the way. Spending time with God is essential to growing and producing great fruit. Reading God's word is a learning experience every day. Why? Because every time you read the Bible, you always get a different outlook on the message.

Let's walk through the steps of taking off the **MASK.**

1. **Admit** you have lied to yourself and others.

2. **Admit** that you need help.

3. **Let go** of success and fame that brought misery and pain.

4. **Confess** what you did to get where you are.

5. **Ask for forgiveness** from the people you have hurt for years.

Your marriage has suffered for years, and your family has been neglected. You have put everything before them and never consider their feelings while climbing the corporate ladder of success. Yes, you made it, but look at the ones you neglected while making it to the top.

They cheered you on. They were confident in who they were becoming, so they supported you with love, spent sleepless nights listening to you prepare your presentation, helped you study, and, most importantly, put your success before their own.

And all along, you lied, deceived, and manipulated all because of greed, envy, jealousy, rejection, control, anger, and the feeling of abandonment.

See, you held on to all the pain that caused you trauma for years, and you covered up the hurt by hurting others. You programmed your mind to hide the shame and guilt by getting whatever you wanted, no matter who was hurt in the process. Over the years of hiding behind the pain, you developed different addictions to find ways to cope with the pain.

Some of those addictions include sex, drugs, pornography, violence, and abuse, and the one that people always overlook is control because it goes unnoticed, and many are unaware of the signs.

Having an addiction to control is a **mask** within itself. I know you are wondering how. I'm glad you asked. When you have on the **mask** of control, you talk good, you sound good, you smell breathtaking, your swag game of style is on fleek, and you walk with a certain aura about yourself when you are masked with control.

Listen to the words of this poem that I know you can relate to in more ways than one.

I wake up hurting mentally. I look in the mirror and see the ugly, unhappy, confused, angry me. I do not like what I see. I hide it with a smile; I hide it with success; I hide with control; I am broken, I am hurt, I am lost.

Trying to understand the voices in my head, not understanding the torment that reminds me of my past daily. Wanting to be free from the anger and torment, I act out in anger, hurting others just to feel comfort.

Trapped in an isolated box, trying to break out of fear of the unknown. I find myself hiding the shame of my past. I feel like no one will understand or want to deal with the scars I hide. I lie just to hide the ugly me.

I deceive others just to hide the broken me. I am addicted to pain because of abuse. I am addicted to sex because of my loneliness. I am addicted to drugs because of the pain.

After all I have tried to do to cope, even wanting to commit suicide, nothing has given me peace or comfort. This is me. I am broken.

When you deal with brokenness, hiding behind a mask of deception, these are feelings you have. Being the real you allows God to heal you, deliver you, and show the world all you have overcome.

Taking off the mask allows God to heal and restore the unique, authentic you who is loved by many. Freedom allows you to live mentally free from the bondage of your past.

Freedom restores the heart; it allows you to forgive all who hurt you, and you can let go and embrace all God has for you. Being free gives you a new outlook on life. You will begin to walk with God-given confidence, knowing that with God, you can do anything.

CHAPTER 6

Knowing Your True Identity

Understanding your purpose requires you to know your true identity in Christ Jesus. Understanding your God-given DNA requires you to live up to a current standard. When you have the DNA of God, it allows you to walk in an unusual, bold anointing.

Understanding your divine purpose for being created sometimes requires you to search deeply within. Experiencing severe trauma will cause you to be confused about your identity.

So many times, people experience rejection by way of what people speak over them because of anger or neglect. Often, we experience an identity crisis as a child trying to understand life. As a child, we learn by hearing different things being said to us and about us, and it develops a mental pattern of what will be produced from our lives.

Words have the power to create life and the power to take life away. When you experience severe trauma, you often feel like there is no hope for a great future or limit your ability to be great.

Not understanding the feeling of abandonment, you begin to develop a thought process of not amounting to anything and not feeling important. When you mentally isolate yourself from reality and the truth of who you are, you begin to feel inadequate and incompetent to live a normal life.

Psalm 147:3 (NIV) says, "He heals the brokenhearted and binds up their wounds."

Overcoming mental torment is not easy, especially when battling all the words you have heard over the years in your mind. Often, people are put in your life to encourage and push you, but sometimes, it is hard to process the great things people say about you.

Not understanding how to process the positive because of years of negativity, you reject the words of encouragement, thinking people have a hidden motive when all along God sent them.

When you are chosen and ordained by God, you have the birthright to inherit the DNA of Jesus Christ.

Allowing God to develop your identity gives you a mind of freedom and a new outlook on your life. Despite the trauma experienced in your life, God can manifest miracles from your testimony. Your life is a book of what God healed and delivered you from. No longer will you walk in shame.

These are some everyday principles concerning your identity.

- Confess daily, "My identity is secure in Jesus."
- I am an overcomer of my past.
- My life is a testimony to healing others.
- I have the DNA of Jesus Christ.
- I have the authority to rule and to reign.

Your identity is what makes you who you are. You often create a false identity to please people and appear to have it all figured out. False identity is when you live life as someone you are not.

Your identity is what displays your character and integrity as a human being. When you falsely deceive others just to feel appreciated, it allows people to see the undeveloped mind of how you think.

There is always a root to every issue you face throughout life, and the root of false identity is deception. Deception is the action of deceiving someone, meaning you deliberately plan your attack before it happens.

When the spirit of deception is in operation, you allow the spirit to control your actions, mood, and, more so, your ability to make wise decisions. When dealing with confusion and trying to understand God's purpose, this prayer reminds you to keep pushing.

Father, I come before You as humble as I know how. I ask You to forgive me of my sins, wash me with your blood, and cleanse me from all unrighteousness.

Father, I ask in Jesus' name to heal my mind and give me wisdom on how to live daily. Guide me through all truths. Lead me daily to see all that is in store for me. In the name of Jesus, I decree and declare I am victorious in You.

Father, thank You for providing my needs. Thank You for loving me when I cannot love myself. I give You total control of my life.

According to Jeremiah 33:6, "Behold, I will bring you health and healing. I will heal them and reveal to them the abundance of peace and truth."

Father, I surrender my will for Your will to be done in my life. I forgive everyone and everything that hurt me and did me harm. I give total access to my thoughts. I give You all of me.

Father, I desire to be healed and restored. I desire to be filled with Your precious Holy Spirit. I give myself away to be used by You, God. Today, I say Yes to Your will for my life. Today, I say Yes to be healed by Your stripes.

Father, for Your word declares in Exodus 23:25, "So shall you serve the Lord your God, and He will bless your bread and Your water. And I will take sickness away from the midst of you."

Father, I thank You for freedom in my mind. I thank You for giving me hope to believe again. Father, I thank You that my true identity rests in You. I give You all the glory and the honor, in Jesus' name.

Amen.

Walking in your true identity with God, you feel peace and security in Christ Jesus. Giving God total control of your life gives you wisdom and knowledge of the heart of God. Spending time in God's presence is an amazing feeling of intimacy unknown to man. Intimacy with God gives you access to the secret place with God. Together, we will see the manifestation of power, authority, healing, and restoration.

CHAPTER 7

Revealing The Real You

Beneath the pain, there is the real you who is ready to break free. For years, the real you has been buried. The unique, funny, talented, intelligent, witty, cool genius has been hidden.

No one really knows who you are.

No one really sees the real you.

Where are you?

I can not see or hear the real you.

Where have you been all these years?

These are some of the things you say to yourself.

I have lost myself in the cares of the world.

I am trying to find myself again. How do I find the real me?

Glad you asked. Finding the real you requires digging deep within to see why the real you was buried for so many years.

The real you was hidden because of the likes of people, wanting to fit in, not liking the unique you, not liking your skin color, not liking your body, not liking your voice, and you spent all this money to build a fake you.

You wasted years of coaching classes to change your voice. You spent a lot of money on cosmetic surgery, implants, etc. You are in debt because of living above your means. You did all you could do for years to fit it, and it still did not work. You are still broken, hiding behind a mask.

For years, you hid from the truth about who you really are.

Why?

Was it because of your career?

Was it because of your friends?

Was it because of your family?

Was it because of shame?

Be truthful with yourself about why you hid all these years.

Brace yourself because the truth can be ugly and scary. Revealing the uncut truth is the only way to be free to be you.

Living a life of freedom and walking in your true identity is a gift from God.

Why?

Glad you asked. Walking in your true identity allows you to develop your own unique character as a man or woman. With God, all things are possible. The things you can do are limitless once you allow God to cultivate your life.

Understand God had an ordained purpose for you long ago before you decided to run away from you.

Running away from you is when you cannot deal with the monster you created. You find ways to adjust your behavior to fit in. You find ways to make others look and feel bad so the spotlight won't be in your face.

Looking inside of you, you feel hopeless, thinking there is no future for yourself. *I have done wrong so many times I do not deserve another chance*. Often, the negative voices you hear in your head are the devil, the father of lies. Understand Satan's will for your life is to destroy you. The objective of Satan is for you to suffer mentally and to be tormented by your past. Living in fear will hinder all that God has promised because of doubt, uncertainty, confusion, and not knowing the outcome.

Holding on to rejection is a major hindrance because you want to be liked and accepted by people who don't care about your well-being or you as a person.

Once you realize that you determine your future and happiness, you will begin to embrace the love of God and heal. Healing starts in the mind. When you have yet to transform your mind, you will forever be bound to your past, and you will never see the future ahead because of unhealed trauma. To embrace your God-given future, you have to be willing to go through the process of healing from past and present trauma. When you allow past trauma to take over your life, you will never clearly see the future God ordained for you.

Being bound is when your past mistakes have consumed your way of thinking and living. You only see through the eyes of pain and deceit. Here are some things to say to yourself to free your mind of torment.

- I love me.
- I adore myself.

- I am perfectly made in my Father's image.

- I am a royal deposit from heaven.

- I am the head of my life.

- I am at peace within myself.

- I will embrace my life.

- I am healed from my past and present mistakes.

- I am a new version of me.

- I am proud of myself.

Once you have transformed your mind, you will begin to see life in a whole new way. Surrendering to God is the key to wholeness and well-being. Let God be God in your life.

The real you is ready to spring forth to accomplish the impossible. God created you to be a leader. God created you to rule and reign.

Hold your head up. You are the son of a king. You are the daughter of a king. You shall inherit the kingdom of God with excellence and poise. Behold, God is doing new things.

You are a royal king/queen. Now, it is time to take the throne. God has prepared you for greatness, and your light will bring forth a great harvest.

Many lives will be changed because of your light. Many lives will be changed because of your strength through God. Boldly confessing and speaking, God has already opened the door. All you have to do is walk through the door.

CHAPTER 8

Transforming Your Mind

Mind: the element of a person that enables them to be aware of the world and their experiences, to think, and to feel, the faculty of consciousness and thought. (Oxford English Dictionary, 2023)

Emotions: a natural instinctive state of mind deriving from one's circumstances, mood, or relationship with others. (Oxford English Dictionary, 2023)

Fear: an unpleasant emotion caused by the belief that someone or something is dangerous, likely to cause pain or a threat. (Oxford English Dictionary, 2023)

Often, we live our lives based on emotions because of insecurities and rejection. Mental emotions are when you have been traumatized by life severely to the point you live every waking day tormented by the pain you endured.

Trying to wrap your mind around the pain, you have no way of understanding how to let go. Mental emotions will have you living a life of low self-esteem, depression, confusion, and isolation from everything and everyone around you.

Not knowing how to express your emotions will cause you to be intimidated by others. You will feel like you are inadequate to think or learn.

You will begin to display odd outbursts and behaviors. Traumatized emotions will have you acting out in anger, rage, control, and manipulation, all for attention and the opportunity to hurt others before they hurt you. That's the whole objective when you are dealing with mental emotions.

Emotional behaviors that are often displayed include:

- Screaming and hollering
- Cursing
- Anger
- Rage
- Confusion
- Control
- Jealousy
- Fear
- Mind control
- Deceit
- Manipulation

These are just a few. You have to speak life to your mind. Understand an idle mind is the devil's playground for the devil to control your thoughts. When you are able to control your thoughts, it gives God access to speak into your life.

Living in fear will paralyze your destiny because of the unknown. Not knowing will cause distraction and delay in what God desires to do for you. The devil's job is to paralyze your mind with confusion because if you are confused about who you are, you will be confused about your purpose in life.

When you are mentally tormented, emotional, and living in fear, you will not see what God sees for your life. When you are emotional, you feed off of negativity, and the more you feed into negative thoughts, you consume your life around doubt, unbelief, control, and anger, all because of the pain that controls your life.

Understand when you cannot control your emotions, they will take over your life mentally, emotionally, physically, and spiritually. Being controlled by emotions, your mind will be unstable, and you will be out of control, walking through life feeling defeated and lost.

Mental emotions will have you feeling like everyone is against you and like everyone is talking about you. Emotions will make you feel isolated.

Fear of being alone will leave you vulnerable and make you settle for whatever comes your way. Developing different soul ties from sex, friendships, and relationships because of loneliness will cause mental torment and psychosis.

Let's walk through the meanings of soul ties and psychosis.

Psychosis: a severe mental disorder in which thought and emotions are so impaired that contact is lost with external reality. (Oxford English Dictionary, 2023)

Soul ties: A spiritual/emotional connection you have to someone after being intimate with them, usually engaging in sexual intercourse. (Oxford English Dictionary, 2023)

Even after intercourse, it is not easy to move on with your life even after years have gone by. Something always draws you back to them by way of a thought or how they made you feel in the moment. Casual sex will make you feel more vulnerable, more open to deception, and more emotional because you think it is love when, all along, it is lust for what you feel.

By giving your body to someone who is not your husband or wife, you give them a valuable piece of you that you will never get back. Casual sex will cause lifetime heartache and pain.

Caught up on the feeling and sensation, you are now trapped by the lust of the eye that seems to you to be love. Not understanding the development of spiritual soul ties, you now feel all the emotions and pain that your partner feels, along with the issues you deal with within yourself.

When you begin to not care about life or how people feel because of your actions, you will seek ways to make them feel less valuable and unworthy. You will begin to control their every move with the way you speak to them or the way you make them feel defeated.

You find ways to dig deep into the heart of the individual to see what makes them vulnerable and open to abuse. When an individual is mentally and emotionally unstable, the individual looks for ways to feel wanted and needed, only to find out it is a mask of what looks like love.

When dealing with mental emotions, you will settle for the abuse mentally, physically, and emotionally. You will settle for the beatings and the late-night phone calls. You will settle for drug usage, you will settle for being the mistress, you will settle for being neglected and rejected, and you will settle for the back and forth in prison or jail, just to name a few. You have to know when it is enough. If you don't stand for something, you definitely will fall for anything that looks, sounds, smells, and tastes good to the flesh.

Pleasing the flesh will cause you to miss what God has ordained for your life. Sacrificing your flesh by praying and fasting will help you to hear God clearly. God will show you who you really are and the things that you need to be delivered from, as well as things that are hindering you.

The awesome thing about fasting is that you deny your flesh in order to receive God's divine will for your life. Denying your flesh increases your spirit to be fed more by God. Allowing God to feed your spirit gives you supernatural wisdom, knowledge, and understanding of how to navigate through this journey called life.

Spending time with God is priceless. There is no other better feeling than feeling the love of God comforting you when you are at your lowest.

Allowing God to transform your life and the way you think will help you to understand the new and improved version of who you have become. After all the years of learning, God taught me in many ways to trust Him.

Trusting God takes a lot of faith and endurance. Even when you do not see what God is doing, you still have to have faith to know everything is working out for your good. Trusting God is an exciting journey because of the unknown.

The most amazing thing about allowing Him total control over your life is that God will always give you nothing but His very best for your life. Here is a prayer that will help you transform the way you see yourself and the way you think.

Father, I come to You as humble as I know how. Father, I thank You for renewing my mind and giving me strength throughout this journey. Father, I decree and declare my mind is whole in You. I speak life to my mind.

I say my mind is hidden in the blood of Jesus. Father, I thank You for taking the scales of my eyes to see what You see about my life. I thank You, Father, for showing me the way. Today, God, I embrace my new mind and identity in Christ Jesus.

Father, I thank You for loving me and giving me peace to know that all things are working for my good. Father, I repent of my sins (call them out). I thank You for washing my sins in the blood of Jesus.

Father, I thank You for giving me a mind of freedom to accomplish the impossible. I know with Your help and guidance, there is nothing I cannot do.

Father, in the name of Jesus, every curse that has been spoken over my life is burned by the fire of Jesus. Holy Spirit, thank You for teaching me how to war over the thoughts in my mind, and I confess I will take control over my mind with the word of God guiding me.

Father, thank You for giving me the courage to speak and confess Your word. Father, I decree and declare in the name of Jesus that I am anointed and appointed by God to do His will on earth as it is in heaven.

Today, I walk in freedom. Today, my mind is restored. Today is a new day. Today, I will see the hand of God move in my life. I will see God move throughout the earth. I confess that I am restored by the fire of God all the days of my life. Amen.

With this prayer, you are going to see wonderful and great things manifest. Pray this daily, and all I can say is, watch God.

CHAPTER 9

Poverty Mindset

Poverty is developed from the co-existence of not knowing who you are in Christ. When searching for a sense of acceptance, you seek and search for validation and affirmation of who you are; not understanding the torment and mental drainage of living someone else's dream or ambitions, you lose a sense of your identity and value.

Poverty is a way of living poorly and lacks stability. You begin to develop poor habits of just living for the moment. You have no dreams, nor do you set goals to accomplish throughout life.

A poverty mindset is developed as a child. You begin to develop a lifestyle that is conducive to your environment. Instead of you living above your environment, poverty gives you a new identity where your environment consumes you.

Being consumed by poverty, you will never see the future clearly. You will always limit yourself, you will label yourself, and you will feel rejected, abandoned, confused, and angry because you have developed a spirit of poverty. Having the mindset of poverty will damage you so severely to the point of no repair.

You go through years of cycles of poor thinking, poor living, and a poor environment where all you know to do to cope is smoke cigarettes, do drugs, lie, sell drugs, manipulate people for your own gain, and have sex with whoever to please an emotional high. This happens all because you have lost your identity living with a poverty mindset.

When you have been damaged since childhood, it is hard to repair the rejection and the abandonment because of the deep-rooted pain that lies within. Dealing with deep rejection and emotional abuse will have you acting out emotionally, and you will begin to blame everyone for your mistakes.

The more you try to get ahead, the more trials and tribulations you have to deal with daily. Being wasted by the destruction of poverty, it is hard to see freedom. It is hard to believe the good within yourself.

So many times, God will send people to you to show you who you are, speak a word, and help you along the way, and yet you still find a way to sabotage all they have sacrificed and invested in you. You will begin to think that working a nine-to-five job forever is a great thing to do while you are feeling trapped in your mind, wondering when you will be free from poverty.

It was never God's intention for you to work and labor hard. God always desired for you to be fruitful and multiply and advance the kingdom of God.

When you understand who you are in God, you will not settle by the standards of man. Once you embrace what God said about you and how great your future is in God, there is nothing you cannot accomplish. Confess this over your life and watch how your mind begins to transform.

My mind is transformed by the power of God.

I am strong in God.

I know how to manage the wealth God gives me.

I am a good steward of my finances.

I am God's inheritance.

I do not have a poverty mindset.

It is God's will for me to be fruitful.

I am the heir of my forefathers, Abraham, Isaac, and Jacob.

My mind is renewed in Christ.

When you cannot see the future for yourself, no one can make the future come to pass but you. We can all pray for you, give you encouraging words, and give you prophecies, but until you see the future, you will forever be stuck in your past, holding on to unforgiveness and guilt for what you did not accomplish. Holding on to guilt will paralyze your future and destiny.

Proverbs 10:15 says, "The rich man's wealth is in his strong city. The destruction of the poor is their poverty."

Romans 3:23-24 says, "For all have sinned, and come short of the glory of God v24 Being justified freely by his grace through the redemption that is in Christ Jesus."

These scriptures let us know that we have all fallen, and it is God's grace and mercy that keeps us from falling deeper into sin. Often, sin can cause us to have a spiritual poverty mindset because we do not see ourselves the way God sees us.

Poverty comes in different forms; it is not limited to just one thing. Poverty is developed from a lack of compassion; you feel like everyone owes you or you feel superior to others.

Poverty is developed by a lack of support. You begin to feel like everyone is against you, and you look at yourself as inadequate to others.

Poverty is developed through the spirit of pride, thinking you are okay and don't need anyone. You feel isolated, not wanting to be around people, or you are always thinking people are out to harm you.

Poverty is developed by your environment, the way you carry yourself, the way you see the world as a whole, the mindset you have about money, and the way you constantly think and act broke.

Dealing with the spirit of pride, you feel like you have arrived and accomplished more than others. You will begin to act like you accomplished it all by yourself, recognizing God and giving God all the glory for your accomplishments. When you do not understand how to deal with a poverty mindset, you will develop coping skills to avoid the root cause of the mindset.

In dealing with the mind, you have to understand the root of what caused you to feel the way you felt. Was it something you saw, something you felt, was it something that happened to you?

Let's find out. Sometimes, throughout life, we overlook the signs of our children crying out, our family crying out, and our friends crying out. We always look at the natural aspect of that individual, not understanding or recognizing the pattern of their thought process.

Not understanding the mind, in silence, you think everything is okay, and no one knows what is going on in the mind.

Not understanding the hurt that is buried because of the abuse causes you to feel isolated. The abuse led to abandonment and rejection. Now that you have all this going on in your environment and your mind, you now develop a poverty mindset where you are now thinking you have to deal with the abuse.

You begin to think about how angry you have become. Once you develop a mindset of abuse because of hurt, you will go through life abusing and hurting people because of anger and isolated thinking of feeling unloved.

Crying inside, and no one sees the pain that is hidden. You act out in pride, you act out in rage, not knowing how to deal with those emotions within, now starving for help and attention.

When dealing with a poverty mindset, the spirit of deception is easy to creep in the front door, side, and back. Dealing with the spirit of deception, you will manipulate and control others because of the neglect that you have experienced.

Experiencing neglect will hurt everyone and everything God sends your way. Why? Because you cannot accept the broken you who is hiding behind a mask.

Taking off the mask will hurt and cause you to deal with the root of your pain. Dealing with the root of pain, you will see the ugly you that has worn a mask for years. You have now developed an identity of an imposter of someone other than you. You created a deceiver who climbed the corporate ladder with the mask and control of deception.

God wants to heal you within for you to produce outer greatness. Once you are healed internally, you develop your identity, and once you heal within, you are now able to embrace your outer by producing a greater future. God is a healer. God wants you to live life abundantly. Allowing God to heal you within gives you the comfort of knowing your true identity.

Dealing with an identity crisis, you cannot see who you are. You only see what you created from hurt and deception. Living a life with a false identity, people will see only the mask that hides the true you. The only way the mask comes off is when you are provoked when you are angered, especially exposure.

Being exposed will become offensive. You will lie, and you will manipulate even more to hide the truth. People will use other people to cover up things hidden within that person.

When deception is exposed, sometimes people deny the fact of seeing the signs and continue to make excuses to others for the behavior of that person. So many times, you know the truth and still deny the truth of what God said and what God is showing you.

Pay attention to the signs. Pay attention to the stop sign. Pay attention to the red light. These all are warnings God is giving you so you can be protected. Understanding who you are, you will not settle for less than what God has for you. God will give you His best, not what is convenient.

So many times, when you think you need something, it is not really what you need. Once you move your flesh out of the way, you can see that person's true spirit. They are either lost trying to find their way, or they refuse to change or whatever the case may be. You have to stay focused on the voice of God for direction. Giving God all of you leaves no room for yourself.

Once you begin to break strongholds off of your mind, you begin to see and hear more effectively. So many times, because of guilt and insecurities, you blame everyone for your issues because you do not want to deal with the real you.

Dealing with the real you can sometimes be uncomfortable. Revealing the hidden things within will cause you to be angry and sad, finding excuses to justify your actions. You will begin to act out in anger because of insecurities and embarrassment of not dealing with personal issues that have held you back for so many years.

The majority of the time, these issues arise as an adult, and you have a hard time understanding how you allowed it to get this out of control, or you begin to ask yourself, why did you hide it for so long? Why did you not seek help before now? All kinds of questions will surface in your mind, going through life for so long thinking you are okay just to find out you are broken and need to be delivered from mental strongholds that have almost cost you your life.

Allowing God total control gives you wisdom unknown to man. Allowing God into your hidden brokenness, hidden insecurities, and hidden trauma gives you room to grow, gives you peace within, gives you the capacity to embrace a great future, and gives you a heart to love again. Now that you are free to live life, let's embrace God's love to live a life of freedom free from poverty. God desires for you to live life healthy, whole, and secure.

Father, I come to You as Your daughter/son. Father, I repent of my sins and call them out. Father, I ask You to wash my mind with the blood of Jesus so I can see my future as You see my future. Father, I decree in Jesus' name that I will live life with a changed mindset and renewed mind. In the name of Jesus, I decree that I will live up to the standards of Christ and not of man.

I decree and declare that my mind is changed and renewed. I now know that I am not subject to my environment, but my environment has changed because of the anointing of the Holy Spirit. Father, thank You for transforming my poverty mindset. Thank You for giving me the inheritance of Your kingdom. Thank You for allowing me to see the fruits of Your kingdom. Father, thank You for teaching me to live the way You desire for me to live.

I decree and declare that the power of Jesus will give me a renewed mind, a renewed spirit, a renewed understanding, and a new identity in Christ Jesus. Today, I embrace the new mindset about wealth. Today, I embrace my new path. Today, I embrace a new version of myself. Today, I no longer hold on to my past. I embrace my future, which is great. Father, I give You all the glory and honor in Jesus' name. Amen.

I decree and declare poverty is not my way of thinking.

I decree and declare I will be fruitful and produce kingdom fruit.

I decree and declare I am God's masterpiece.

I decree and declare I am God's mouthpiece on the earth.

I decree and declare I will not compromise the gospel of Jesus Christ.

I decree and declare I have the DNA of my Father, God.

I decree and declare I will remain humble while God is glorified.

I am a royal priest.

I am victorious in Christ Jesus.

I have the mantle of Deborah.

I have the mantle of Joseph.

I have the mantle of Issac.

I have the mantle of Jeremiah.

I will take rebuke and correction with love from God's vessels.

I will hold on to God's words spoken over my life. I am healed by the blood of Jesus. I am strong and mighty with the help of Jesus. I will stand tall with the healing power of Jesus. It has given me the courage to speak. I am given the confidence to do His will. I am sent by God throughout the earth. I will set boundaries. I will not compromise for fame and money.

Hold your head up and know that you will see the glory of God in your life.

CHAPTER 10

Choices Can Be A Hindrance Or A Blessing

In life, we all have to make decisions. We have to make a decision about our career path. We have to make a decision on our job.

The remarkable thing about God is He gives us choices to make, and we have to decide what is best with the help of God. Understand when God is the head of your life, you have to let God take control of everything about your life.

Making a decision, you choose the path you want for your life. If you feed your mind with deception, lies, manipulation, and control, these are the behaviors you will see displayed throughout your life. When living a toxic life, you affect the people around you to the point they become accustomed to the abuse in many ways.

Some people get a high from inflicting pain on others. Making people feel inferior to you gives you the power to mind control everything about the individual.

They will begin to feel as if they cannot make a decision without your approval.

You will begin to see familiar patterns throughout their life that will have you questioning, are they living their lives through me?

Why? Because, for one, they envy you and your life. Two, they feel less than to accomplish their dreams. Third, you did everything to tear down their spirit so that they no longer believe they can accomplish anything.

Being a failure is all they think about. Trying to understand the mind and behavior of others cannot be done out of emotions because emotions will cause you to feel the pain that was afflicted. Emotions will have you feeling isolated and confused. Emotions will have you thinking about ways to retaliate.

When you act out of emotions, you do not make accurate decisions.

Emotions will have you settling and compromising the anointing on your life just to feel worthy, loved, accepted, confirmed, and filling a void of loneliness.

Holding on to fleshly desires will lead you to a road of confusion of an illusion of truth, only to find out it is a lie from hell to destroy your life. Allowing God to cultivate your life, your emotions will align with the will of God, where it will work for your good.

Understand when you are not healed, you are open to deception because of vulnerability. When your spirit is open, the enemy sets a plot for an attack on the weak areas in your life. Understanding God gives you signs and warnings before you have a head-on collision.

You often ignore the signs and compromise the truth for an illusion. Once the illusion comes to manifestation, you are now being blindsided by the enemy that you did not see because of emotions, pride, betrayal, confusion, doubt, anger, etc. All of these plots were to set you up for destruction.

You have a choice to surrender to the will of God totally. You have a choice to stay bound. You have a choice to be free. God gives you free will and choice. God will always give you a way of escape. It is up to you to choose your path and destiny.

Making decisions sometimes requires you to dig deep past your emotions and what they look like. When you begin to feel pressure, push past the pain and choose to worship God in the pain. Choose to give God praise.

Even in the pain of crying and screaming, allow God to dig deep to be free. Sometimes, you have to go as far back as childhood to uproot the past hurt that you have chosen to stop your destiny. Give it to God and make a choice. Here are some things you can speak to your spirit daily.

- God's love is great.
- God's love is true.
- God's love is whole.
- God's love is forgiving.

Redirecting your thought process is essential to your destiny and healing. When you realign your mind with the things of God, you have to feed your spirit with scripture and powerful words to change your mindset. So, by all means, as I put these quotes or words in the blueprint, read them daily and watch God transform your life. If God did for me, He will do it for you.

- God has a purpose for my life.
- I am chosen to be great.
- God is love. God is peace. God is joy.
- I am mentally free.
- I have the mind of Christ Jesus.
- I am free from bondage.

CHAPTER 11

The Unknown

It's okay to feel scared. It's okay to be cautious. Understand you are safe in God's arms.

I know over the years, you got caught up with the cares of the world and forgot about what was important. You get so consumed with family, friends, making money, and traveling that not many times do you consider just slowing down and reflecting on the good things of God. Often, throughout life, you forget how you accomplished success. It was God who blessed you to be a doctor, lawyer, judge, or nurse. It was God who gave you the strength to conquer the impossible. So many times, people forget the process and the blood, sweat, and tears. When it is all said and done, God is all we have.

It was God who gave you a chance to change the lives of others. You are a blessing to help others. You are the lifeline. Many sick people put their lives in your hands. God gave His son Jesus for you to live through the blood of Jesus.

You are the DNA of Jesus. Jesus made a sacrifice so you could live a life of freedom. The unknown is an uncomfortable place because you are not in control. Everyone cannot see the vision within you. Allowing the unknown to cultivate your life to accomplish the impossible is amazing.

The unknown will give you access to places unknown to man. God loves us so much that He will take you away from everything just to set you up for success, wealth, good health, and divine favor with God and man.

When you obtain favor with men, you get access to rooms with great men and women. God's love is so great. There is no other love that can compare to the love of God. When you allow God to take over your life, there is nothing that can stop God's will for you.

Holding on to the wisdom of God will take you to unknown territory where you will conquer the miraculous. Living in the system of God, you have an advantage in staying ahead of the game.

God is so awesome. He gave us the power to dominate in the marketplace. We were created to rule and reign in the marketplace. The takeover anointing will cause people to come to you for answers.

Remaining humble to God and in His will allows you to forever move by the beat of God's rhythm. Worship creates an atmosphere for God to dwell and speak clearly. God will speak with you. God will guide you. God will show you. God will teach you. God is your counselor. You will give you God-ordained wise counsel.

The unknown will allow you to make history for God to tell His story through you. Let me share a testimony with you. I traveled for five years of my life on the road as a travel nurse. God allowed me the opportunity to travel all over the world. I was making great money and meeting great people. I knew

God had a greater purpose for my life. I got comfortable, and I enjoyed traveling and doing what I love to do, which is travel, not understanding that my purpose was better than traveling and working for someone else. When the pandemic hit, I was like, *okay, God, what am I going to do now?* God allowed the pandemic to slow us down. I understood I was making money and traveling, but I got too busy to spend time with God. I got consumed with working. God always has a way of getting your attention.

I came back home in July of 2020, and I was devastated because I was so used to traveling. It took me a long time before I just surrendered to God's will for why I came off the road. What made it more interesting was that God sent me back to the place where it all started. I had to go home to Alabama. *Oh my God, I had a hard time with that adjustment.*

I started a job in September, and I only worked there for four months. One night, God told me it was time, and I immediately put my resignation letter in for submission. I then began to wonder, *what are You doing, God?* I began to think about all the things that could go wrong because I was used to making money like I wanted, and I was comfortable.

One night, I was crying out to God and just sharing my heart about Him telling me to leave my job. God said, "My daughter, I allowed you to travel to show how great it would be working for me. I want to give you great wealth that man cannot give you." I made the money, and the quicker I made it, the quicker it was leaving my hands. God was telling me, "Daughter, I want you to live a life of freedom and travel while making money doing what you love, and that is coaching and mentoring people to greatness."

God had already ordained me to be a life coach and mentor while traveling. God was building my character while traveling. God was allowing me to set people free while traveling.

I was coaching people on how to do different things with their lives, and I did not even know it. It was easy for me to come up with a conspiracy for them to be free. It was all God for me to be where I am today. I did not understand what I needed during the most important time ever.

The pandemic caused a lot of people to lose themselves through the transition of losing everything that they worked so hard to accomplish. I had to go through the process of being rejected by man, but I now know that my love comes from God, who will always see the good in me. God is my number one supporter, fan, and cheerleader, and He pushes me to greatness.

What I love so much about God is even when I become fearful about not working, He reminds me that I am destined for greatness and that He has my back every step of the way.

Holding to every word God speaks to you will give you the confidence to conquer the impossible with boldness. The unknown will open the heavens on your behalf just because you trusted God to do it for you even when you did not see the way. Hearing what God said and seeing what God said has to meet destiny and purpose. They have to become one to succeed in the unknown.

Pray this prayer daily.

Father, I come in the name of Jesus as Your daughter/son. Father, I ask You to guide me through the unknown. Father, I thank You, Jesus, for giving me direction on how to trust You even more.

Father, I will forever surrender to Your will for my life. I thank You, Father, for peace unknown to man.

Father, I repent of my sins and call them out to God. I thank You for forgiving me as I lay myself at the feet of Jesus. I thank You for an understanding of the unknown. Father, I thank You for this wonderful journey that You have given me to travel, and I will embrace Your love and protection as I dwell in Your secret place.

Father, I give You all the glory for my accomplishments. I give You all the glory for allowing me to do Your will on earth as it is in heaven. Father, I love You, and I bless You forever. In Jesus' name. Amen.

CHAPTER 12

Arise and Soar

Knowing who you are in God gives you confidence, boldness, and courage to conquer the impossible. Walking boldly in your calling gives you a new outlook on life and all that you can accomplish. There are no limits in the kingdom of God. It is time to arise and let your light shine within. Many were thinking you would fail. Many did not see the masterpiece God kept hidden.

No one knows that the roar of your voice will shake the nations. No one knows the purpose that awaits you. Arise! You are ready to soar. No longer will you flock with pigeons. No longer will you sit amongst ravens. No longer will you lay with chickens.

It is time to soar high as God gives you the wisdom to conquer the impossible. Stand tall and know that your time has come when many will marvel over what God has done in you and through your life.

Embrace the new you.

Embrace the marvelous wonders that have manifested with the love of God.

God knew you were destined to be great. That's why it took years to discover you. You were a masterpiece unfolding before the eyes of men.

No one knew the path that awaited you. They all talked and guessed, but no one knew. Not even your closest friend could get the credit for this masterpiece.

God ordained you before the foundation of the world. You are more ready than you know. Until you unleash the roar, you will never know the authority you possess. Open your mouth and sound the alarm.

The time has come to unleash the roar of deliverance and breakthrough. Giving God all of you has granted you access to limitless possibilities with His stamp of approval.

Giving God all of you has opened up heaven's treasure over your life. Giving God all of you has allowed you access to the impossible with the favor of God in your life. Arise and soar. The nations are ready, the regions are ready, the cities are ready, and Wall Street is ready.

God did not forget about you. So many times, because of your guilt and insecurities, you blame everyone for your issues because you do not want to deal with the real you.

You are your worst enemy. When people see greatness in you, you find a way to speak negatively about yourself and do not listen to the voice of God speaking. As believers and non-believers, we have to make up our minds that we want more out of life so we can see all that God has to offer us.

Ask God to guide you and show you what is hindering your path to greatness. It is time to rise up and stop throwing a pity party because of your defeat or struggles. Yes, it hurts.

Yes, you failed the test a couple of times. Yes, I know you feel like you are not educated enough.

Okay, now that you have cried and repented, let's move on so you can walk boldly and confidently into your purpose and watch God be great in your life. God desires for you to be great. Throughout the Bible, God talks about being greater because that is what He desires from His children.

You were God's son or daughter before you were created. So think about it: who do you owe your life to before anything else?

You owe God your life. He gave you the gift of life. God gave access to heaven to experience the joy of the Lord through the good and the bad. Throughout my journey of deliverance, every day, I would write different quotes that would help me on days I was struggling to get it together.

I would write quotes that would encourage my spirit and who God said I was to Him. Understand it is important to feed your mind with the thoughts of God and His promises. This helped me when I had nothing else to turn to. When I could not even pray for myself, these encouraging quotes helped me through the rough days.

Understanding and maintaining freedom requires sacrifices and determination. You have given up a lot of things that will upset your flesh. You have to let go of your desires and wants.

Your primary focus is on what you need and what is healthy for your mind. The world we live in today always wants it quick. Not many people are willing to go through the process of healing to see greatness manifest in their lives.

When God ordains your life to be great, you will go through a rough season to make you great for His purpose. Allow God to do what He wants to do with your life.

It is all worth it. One of my favorite scriptures is Mark 8:36, "For what shall it profit a man (woman) if he (she) gains the whole world and loses his/her soul." It is amazing how so many well-known believers have given their souls to the devil for the gain of money and fame.

When you have a real relationship with God, no amount of money can turn you away from the love of God. If God be for you, who can be against you?

There is definitely no compromise when it comes to God. I cannot be bought. I have my own wealth; God gave it to me. I didn't have to do something strange for some change. Lord, have mercy on your people.

Here are some ways not to compromise the soar and things to remember.

- Pigeons cannot soar.
- Chickens cannot fly high.
- Low-level thinking will have you bound and low.
- You do not fit in with the crowd.
- Everyone cannot go with you.
- Snakes have no gravity in the air (you are in control).
- Worship will advance you on earth.
- Possess the supernatural favor of God.

- Everywhere you go, let them know God gave you your own money. You do not need their money. You cannot be bought.

- Speak bold.

- Speak the word that God gave you to speak.

When you soar, you do not have to compromise who you are when God has given you boldness and clarity.

When you do what God says and stand on the truth of God, there will be nothing that stands in the way of what God is doing in your life.

When you make God your center of attention and focus, you will ascend to higher levels you can't even imagine.

Hold on to God and watch God do the impossible. God is the source. God is the answer. God is the truth and the light. God is the number one influencer. God is the great I am.

CHAPTER 13

New Beginnings

Now that you have established your identity in Christ Jesus, you do not think the same, you do not act the same, nor do you hang around the same people because of elevation and promotion.

God has given you the power to create a great future with the creative mind that He has given you.

New beginnings will burst out of nowhere because of the strength God has given you within. New beginnings will open many doors. New beginnings will give you access to many opportunities with people of well-known influence.

The key is to keep your foundation clear and zone-free with God. So many people forget that the best Creator and the one true source of hope is God.

God has created so many millionaires, and once they made it popular and famous, they forgot He made it all happen. So many times, people get caught up in the hype of people and attention while compromising the anointing and calling on their lives.

The key is always to keep God first and always keep a low and humble posture.

Here are some ways to stay close to God even when God makes your name great.

- Always remain in a posture of prayer and worship.
- Always be willing to allow God to mold you into greatness.
- Always be willing to grow in God.
- Always come to God as a little child.
- Always glorify God for making it happen.

New beginnings do not involve the opinions of other people. Focusing on God and why He made you are the most important things to focus on.

People pleasing season is over because all the time you were struggling and going through hurt and tournament, none of the people were there with you. When you are created to influence people, you do not go looking for the approval of others.

Holding on to the word God has spoken over your life is the very thing that is going to get you through many doors. Stop looking for everyone to approve of what God said.

When new beginnings take place in your life, you cannot tell everyone your dreams and visions. Everyone cannot see the vision that God gave you. Hold on to the faith of God, and He will make a way for you.

CHAPTER 14

The Mask Of Deception

Once God has revealed the secret to your defeat, it is now up to you to pray to God for strategies to demolish the stronghold that has held up your identity. One thing about God is that He will never force you to choose right or wrong.

God will always give you a choice. So many people deal with deception willingly because of a comfortable and familiar place of liking the attention.

Some people get used to the lies and failures of others. So many people like to see people vulnerable and weak, which gives them the power to manipulate and control their minds.

Throughout life, I dealt with all types of hurt and deceit from church friends, family, and supposed-to-be loved ones.

I suppressed my pain for years and hid behind drugs, men, sex, money, and fame, all to discover I was dealing with the spirit of deception. Why? People would see me one way: praising God, praying for people, setting people free from demonic strongholds, and no one realized I had a stronghold of deception and the only person who could set me free was God.

After years of living in deception, one night, I was lying in bed, and I heard the voice of God say to me clearly, "I chose you, but you are a liar, you are deceitful, you are a manipulator, and you control my sons and daughters by pleasing their flesh."

God said to me that night that if I did not repent and seek Him for help, I would suffer severely. I would be exposed before many, so He advised me to come to the throne of grace to be healed. Understand before God exposes you and causes severe chaos, He warns you first.

So many lie and say, "Oh, God, does not expose people." Or they say, "It is not God's will for you to be exposed." so many times, people hide behind the scripture to make it seem like God is a liar and what they are doing is right. News flash! You are wrong, and your flesh needs to be checked before God exposes your mess.

Hiding behind a mask of false identity, you will always pretend to be something that you are not. Creating a false identity leads to deception, where you become controlled by the life of someone else. This means you build your whole life around a lie or pretend to have it all together when, all along, you are broken, hurt, confused, and robbed of your true identity. People see you healing, preaching, flowing in the gifts, and all along, the gift cannot destroy the strongholds and struggles you deal with daily.

The only thing that can destroy yokes and lift burdens is the true authentic anointing of God's chosen, and you wonder why no deliverance is taking place. No oil!! When you carry the oil, true healing and deliverance take place.

Hiding behind the spirit of deception will have you thinking the power of God is moving only for the truth to be revealed of deceit. When walking in deceit, you manipulate people for your own accomplishments and benefit.

The spirit of deception causes people to have a mental breakdown of the way they see themselves and others. People can be so mentally disturbed that they will live the life of someone else, talk the way they do, and tell God's people all kinds of false lies and prophecies, all to find out they tapped into your future from terror cards, palm reading, voodoo dolls, enchantments, physics, etc.

When the spirit of deception is in full operation through people, they will shout, scream, run, lay hands, speak in tongues, and everything you can think of, all for the attention of the people. So when you are at your lowest, vulnerable state of mind, they can tell you all the sweet, empty lies you want to hear, all to feed off of your emotions and drop you spiritually.

Deception has all kinds of avenues and detours before it gets to the right destination. Once the spirit has arrived at the destination, there are more friends along for the ride who are ready to feed off the prey of the weak. Behind deception, you have pride, anger, rage, control, manipulation, jealousy, lying, and a sneaky peek-a-boo spirit.

When dealing with deception, you come in contact with all types of spirits, and the only way you can see them is when you have a gift to see in the spirit realm. Everyone is not able to operate in the capacity to see principalities, witches, and warlocks.

Everyone does not have the authority to go into certain realms of the spirit. You have to be summoned to enter certain realms of the spirit, and that is only given by God, releasing certain chosen ones with authority to operate in the capacity.

Surrendering to the will of God gives you access to His voice and direction. When God can trust you, He gives you certain gifts and teaches you how to handle what He has given you.

Understand when dealing with deception, you have to have eyes to see beyond what you see in the natural. When dealing with different spirits, you have to allow your spirit and discernment to take over your natural thought process.

For years, many have been deceived by the lust of the eye, wanting more fame at all costs, wanting the attention of the rich and famous, and willing to sell their soul at any cost.

So many have lost sight of their true ordained purpose of why they were created on the earth. The spirit of deception makes the truth look like a lie, and the lie looks like the truth. Many cannot distinguish between the two, all because of the ignorance of the fleshly desires.

Lost and trapped in a society where any and everything is accepted, many have found themselves accepting the abuse, being rejected, and being abandoned. Many have adapted to being deceived.

They think it is the normal way of living in the world today, not understanding that the seasons change in nature as well as in the spirit. Many people are not prepared or ready for the shift as the season changes.

Pay attention to the winter season. You have new relationships on the rise. You have new businesses on the rise. You have new ministries on the rise. There are a lot of things happening in this particular season during the winter.

Now, here comes the fall season. Everything is blossoming very well, and everyone is happy with their family, business, etc. Suddenly, out of nowhere, there comes an interruption of plans again, and everyone is caught off guard.

No one took heed to the signs and warnings of what was coming in the day ahead. Now, everyone is wondering what the next move of God is. Understand God will always prepare His children. God will always speak through the mouth of the prophets who will speak the truth.

Deception has had people blinded for years. Mental illness has different elements that trigger different behaviors. I guarantee you that you have dealt with mental illness in some type of way, and it has gone unnoticed.

I spent five years of my life living in deception, thinking I was okay. I was mentally ill on so many levels. I thought I had it all together and no one would notice my struggles because I masked them so well.

God gave me a prayer about deception so I could be free and able to see the root cause of deception and why I was blinded by the stronghold of deception that had taken my identity.

Father God, I come to You humble, and I lay myself at Your feet to hear Your voice. Father, I need Your help. I am broken. I am confused. I feel abandoned, rejected, and unworthy of God.

I need Your help. Father, help me to see the deception that had me blinded. I have spent my life in deception. God deliver me from the hands of the enemy. I need Your blood, Jesus, to set me free. Father God, for years, I have hidden behind sex, lying, manipulation, control, pride, drugs, masturbating, deceit, backbiting, envy, and jealousy.

God, I want to surrender my will to Your will. Jesus, I need the blood to heal me as I cry out to You. Father God, I know that there is power in Your son Jesus' name. I need the power of Jesus to heal and deliver me from the strongholds of my mind.

Deliver me from myself. Father God, help me to trust Your word to know that Psalm 91 will protect me from my enemy.

Father, I cry out to You. I don't know what else to do but cry out for help to save my soul from damnation.

Father God, I ask You to break the stronghold of deception off my life so I can see the hidden root. Reveal to me, God, what is the root cause of deception.

Reveal to me, God, what is trying to take my identity. Father, I give my life to You. I give You control of my life. Father, I yield my will to Your will, and I thank You in advance that I am delivered and set free to live in my God-ordained purpose.

I give myself away for Your glory. I will forever give You all the glory and honor in Jesus' name. I pray to you. Amen.

I prayed that prayer every day, and each day, I saw the root of the spirit of deception. I saw where I allowed the spirit to take over.

The spirit entered from abuse, rejection, and abandonment. I suffered so much trauma, and I was vulnerable to anything that sounded good because I had no prayer life, and I wanted whatever quick fix to take the pain away.

Another way deception came in was by way of wanting attention. I always wanted to feel important, like everyone needed me. I had to be the center of attention.

Deception is a powerful force that will have you thinking you can take over the world and have everyone fall weak and vulnerable to you. It was easy for the spirit of deception to take over because I was always a leader. I was never a follower, so I knew it would be easy to take over weak-minded people.

I saw myself spinning out of control. I knew if I didn't make a conscious decision to change, I was headed for destruction. I gave God my whole heart, and I cried out for help and deliverance because I knew it was my only source of help and comfort.

So many times, you feel like you don't need help, or you think you got it all figured out because you get what you want when you want it, not understanding God sees and knows all things. Soon, it will all come to an end. It is your choice how you determine your end.

CHAPTER 15

God's Chosen

Trying to understand the path God has you on will sometimes seem like a desert where you are all alone.

God is stretching you so you propel at a higher level. Not knowing the direction, you have to build your faith to trust God even when it seems like nothing is happening.

Hold on to what God spoke over your life. Hold on to what God told you in your time of prayer. Hold on to what God ordained before the foundation of the world. You were born to do great things.

I know it seems as if you are failing all tests or you feel like nothing is working for you. Trust me, God is working it all out even when it seems impossible, or you think like you are not worthy.

When God chooses you to do the work, it is an honor because many are called, but there are very few who are chosen to do what He ordained for you to do.

You are special to God to be chosen. It is an honor to be a vessel God uses throughout the earth. Even when you do not understand the plan or your purpose, trust God. He is the author and finisher of your faith. He has everything in control.

In life, you question why there is so much happening that you have no control over. Well, the answer is yes, you have control over a lot that happens in your life.

Life is made up of choices, and you have the right to choose your path in life. What do you desire for your life? How do you want to live your life? Do you desire to be happy? Are you comfortable with your life the way it is?

These are some serious questions you have to ask yourself and be honest with yourself. This is something many people often think about on a daily basis.

God always gives you choices, and it is up to you what you decide. Choosing to serve God is a benefit of eternal life and life more abundantly.

Allowing God to have total control and access to your life is a phenomenal way to experience God's love and faithfulness. Studying the word of God is the blueprint for God's heart and thoughts about His children and the people in the world.

Dealing with the mind includes a wide variety of topics because it can go from having a mind of Christ to having an idle mind, to having a tormented mind, to having a confused mind, to being double-minded, and the list goes on.

So many people think they have no control over their minds. That is a lie because everyone has control over their mind. The problem is what you feed your mind. What you feed your mind will produce in your actions, your everyday life, and how you view people and the world.

Your thoughts play an important role in how your future is shaped and transformed. When you feed your mind negativity, you will produce negativity.

When you feed your mind on the things of flesh, you become emotionally high off of what feels good to your flesh. When you feed your mind fear, you will feel like you are inadequate to accomplish your goals and dreams.

When you feed your mind with the feelings of being rejected and abandoned, you will never feel worthy of love or confident that you deserve love. What do you want for your life?

How do you see yourself ten years from now? What are some goals you have accomplished? Below are some things that will help you focus on who you are as a person. Go over this every day, every night, every minute, every hour, and whenever you need to speak it over your life.

- I will accomplish my dreams.
- I am able to conquer the impossible.
- I am strong in God.
- God has a purpose for my life.
- I am worthy.
- I am confident.
- I am beautiful/handsome.
- I am worthy of love.
- My future is bright.
- I see greatness in myself.
- I see success in myself.
- I am who God says I am.
- God is my Father.

- Today, I confess Jesus as my Lord.

Understand what you speak by faith will come to pass. Faith is what you are hoping for when you do not see it.

Faith moves God to do the impossible. Walking by faith is not what you see but what God spoke over your life. Frequently, throughout my journey with God, I would sometimes feel like, *God, how can I do this? This is too big for me.* But what I had to realize is that it was not about how I was going to do it; it was all about how God was going to do it through me. It was all God's plan, and I am just the vessel for God to move through to do His work.

When you are willing to be used by God, there are no limits to what God will do through you. Spending quality time with God is how we get understanding and revelation on how He wants to use us throughout the earth. Being chosen by God is a phenomenal thing to experience because you gain access to the unknown mysteries of heaven. You get to spend quality time with your Father. You get to see God in a whole new way of intimacy. Yes, you have challenges that come your way, but with God guiding you and giving you instructions and directions, there is nothing you cannot overcome.

Here is a prayer that will help you to navigate throughout your journey.

Father, I come to You humble with a heart of repentance. Father, I thank You for life and life more fruitful according to Your will. Father God, we thank You in the name of Jesus for giving us faith to know we can accomplish the impossible with Your help and guidance. Father, thank You for giving me the understanding of having a surrendered heart. I decree and declare that I will do

Your will on the earth as You have chosen. I thank You, Jesus, for souls being saved, set free, and delivered from my testimony. Father, I give You a surrendered yes. Father, I decree and declare in the mighty name of Jesus that the people I come in contact with will see Jesus, and they will know Jesus. I will speak what you say and move how you want me to move as You choose. Father, I decree in the name of Jesus that I will manifest the will of the Father on earth as it is in heaven. I thank You, Father, for being chosen. I thank You, Father, for choosing me to do your will. Father, I will forever give you all the glory and honor in Jesus' name. Amen.

CHAPTER 16

The Struggle Is Real

So many times, it is hard to overcome certain situations. I know it seems like no one understands what you are going through.

You are not alone. You will get through this with help and guidance. So many of you have suffered verbal abuse from family that was close and dear to your heart. It has caused so much damage and trauma that it is hard for you to live a normal, healthy life.

Growing up abused, all you know throughout life is abuse and hurt. So many people can only function when getting abused. If they are not getting cussed out or beaten, they will find ways to act out to get knocked upside the head.

They will act out to get abused emotionally. When you adapt to toxic behavior and toxic people, you will develop toxic traits where people only see the negative, even when you are trying to do good. Sowing seeds of toxic behavior grows and grows until you can no longer contain the growth. So many people can only function in a toxic relationship or friendship.

They like mental abuse. They like the highs and lows. They like the attention just to say *I got somebody no matter how they treat me. I am broken, but I am comfortable with the abuse that makes me feel special.*

I hid the trauma I suffered silently for many years. Could anyone see or hear my silent cry? I was hurt beyond repair.

The struggle is real when you allow the world to shape and form your life. The struggle is real when you develop emotional soul ties over the years. I know you wonder why you feel depressed and confused.

Let me help you. You developed soul ties over the years with different men and women the other person was involved with, and you now have to suffer the mental abuse and trauma that has nothing to do with you.

Have you ever wondered why you all of a sudden feel heavy and weighed down out of nowhere? Have you ever wondered why you feel oppressed or angry out of nowhere?

Have you ever thought about why you cannot break free from the relationship even when you know they are toxic?

What is keeping you there is the soul ties developed from having sex and not getting married. You gave your body to someone who was not worthy, nor did they deserve to open your treasure box.

Everything is a choice, and you have to come to the point where you get tired of what you are familiar with and comfortable with just to fill the void of loneliness and insecurity.

According to the word of God, in 1 Corinthians 3:6-9 God says one plants, one waters, and God will get the increase. My assignment is to give you the material to guide you through healing and deliverance. It is up to you to decide what you want to do with your life.

The cards will always be in your hand until you allow them to play your hand against you. Don't get so caught up on the emotional high that you lose yourself playing with your life. Below are some steps that helped me when I was battling mentally in my mind.

- I want what God has for me.
- I want God's best.
- I am the apple of God's eye.
- I am a king.
- I am a queen.
- God will guide me and lead me.
- I am strong.
- I have the power to change.
- I want to accomplish great things.
- I am intelligent.
- I am creative.
- With God, all things are possible.
- God, you are my strength.
- Thank you, God, for loving me.

These are some things that helped me along my journey. So many people were praying for me and encouraging me, and I had to decide what I wanted with my life. I wanted more. I knew that God was the only answer and the only help that would free my mind from all the mental trauma. God is the key.

Friends did not have an answer. Pastors did not have time. Family always finds ways to talk about you and your past.

So, the only person I knew who always had a listening ear to hear my plea was God, the Creator.

God knows everything about you. Why? Because He created you in His image. I am going to write you two prayers that will help you through your process. Read them as often as you need to.

Father, in the name of Jesus, I come to You, humble and sincere. Father, I need Your help and guidance. I have done things and said things that are not pleasing to You.

I have given my body to so many different men and women. Father, help me to forgive all who hurt me (call out names). Father, I thank You for Your healing power.

I thank You for taking time out to see about me. I need You, Jesus. I need You to show me the way. Father, I thank You for delivering me from all soul ties and generational curses.

Father, I plead the blood of Jesus over my body. Father God, guide, shield, and protect my body. God, I give my body to you. Make me whole in the blood of Jesus.

I decree and declare I will wait on you, God, to give me Your very best. I know, Father, that You only give the best gifts to Your children who love You and are obedient. God, I want to please You. I want to make You happy with my life.

Today, I give You all my worries, my insecurities, my mind, my body, and my soul. God, thank You for a mind of freedom. God, I want to forever serve You with all of my heart. God, I thank You for making all things new in my life. God, I will forever glorify You and exalt Your name. You saved me.

You loved me enough to send me help. I am forever thankful to You. God, I thank You for the newness I will forever walk in daily. I love You. I adore you, in Jesus' name. Amen.

CHAPTER 17

Loving You Matters

Often, throughout life, we give love to everyone and everything but ourselves. We neglect the most important person that matters. So many have become accustomed to adapting to everyday life and forget to take time out for self-care. Life happens to us all, but we must always take time out for ourselves for so many reasons. Some are going through the process of healing, some are still broken from past relationships, some are trying to figure out life and how to cope with fitting in with society, and some are adjusting to married life and children while dealing with postpartum depression.

Some have lost their identity, pretending to be someone they are not just to be seen and heard. So many people have all this going on. Now you see why it is important to love on you so you can truly heal and operate at your full potential throughout the earth. People often neglect the responsibility to deal with the hurt that is buried within just to fill the void with anything that makes them feel good for the time being.

Pain has many ways of hiding itself.

When you feel unworthy of love, there is some hidden pain and trauma that has gone on for so long that you find ways to forget it ever happened. The thing is, the pain never goes away. All you did was mask the pain so you would not feel it. You masked it with sex, drugs, drinking, pills, overworking, ministry, business endeavors, or whatever you find as your pleasure. The way you see yourself matters. When you value yourself, everyone will see the value in you, and they will value you as well. Love yourself enough to heal from all the trauma that has had you bound for five, ten, fifteen, or twenty years of your life.

Love yourself enough to go through the process of healing. Love yourself enough to allow God to transform your life. Love yourself enough not to settle for less than what God has for you. Now, it is time to know that your identity is in God. God is your only source. He has everything you need in Him. No man, no woman, no job, and no money can compare to the love of God. No matter how you may feel, no matter how you see yourself right now, God is able to do the impossible. When you love yourself, you will transform your mind on how you see yourself and how you view the things in this world. As you read this, I want you to ask yourself some real questions, and when you answer these questions, I want you to transform your thought process about how you see yourself as well as how you feel about yourself. Ask yourself these questions.

- Do I really love myself enough to set boundaries?
- Do I love myself enough to change my environment as well as my circle of friends?
- Do I love myself enough to let them go?
- Do I love myself enough to get out of that abusive relationship?
- Do I love myself enough to seek help?

- Do I love myself enough to face the trauma and deal with it?

- Do I see myself healed and whole?

- What is hindering me from seeing greatness within myself?

- What is causing me to settle for the abuse, the rejection, being the side chick, doing drugs, being an alcoholic?

- Why do I think I am unworthy of love?

As you write down different things that cause you to lose yourself, I want you to write down how you will take time out for yourself throughout the week, month, and year. Set aside time just for you. When you begin to put yourself first, you will begin to make better choices, and you will be mentally grounded to make decisions not based on emotions. When you begin to spend quality, intimate time with God, it gives you security and protection to understand the path God has set before you without fear. Fasting, praying, and worship are essential to a closer relationship with God. There is a difference between a relationship and just church.

Recite this every day, all day, whenever you need encouragement. Whenever you are feeling depressed or overwhelmed, speak this over yourself.

I love myself.

I will set boundaries.

I choose me.

I will take care of myself.

I will love myself enough to heal.

I will not settle.

I will give myself nothing but the best.

I deserve God's love.

I AM God's daughter/son.

I know I AM loved by God.

God is with me always.

I AM the apple of God's eye.

Understand no amount of fame or fortune can compare to God's unconditional love. Yes, you may think there is something greater because of this deceitful world we live in, but I guarantee you that when it is all said and done, the world has no answers or solutions to what has been plaguing your mind for so many years. Love yourself enough to be free from the bondage. Your children want to see you happy. In order to love your children unconditionally, you have to be set free, healed, and delivered so you can love them the way God loves His children.

Luke 18:16-17 says, "Jesus called them unto Him, and said, suffer little children to come to me, and forbid them not for of such is the kingdom of God. Verily I say unto you, whosoever shall not receive the kingdom of God as a little child shall in no wise enter therein."

God loves His children. The Bible tells us to come to God as a child. Why? Glad you asked. God's children are innocent and pure; they do not have hidden motives or agendas. They are always themselves, never pretending. When something hurts them, they cry and run to their dad for help. Unlike grown adults, they find ways to avoid running to God instead of dealing with the pain. Love yourself enough to deal with it; run to God for help.

Let's pray.

Father, in the name of Jesus, I come to You as Your daughter/son. Father, I repent of my sins (call all of them out), and I ask You to forgive me as I turn away from the temptation of sin. Father, I ask You to make me whole as Your son/daughter. I want to be renewed in Christ Jesus. Father, thank You for loving me through the process of healing. I run to You, Father, to heal my hurt. I run to You, Father, to heal me from the abuse. Father, I thank You for protecting me, and I will forever know that Psalm 91 covers me. Father, thank You for restoring my mind, body, and soul. I decree and declare I am healed, I am set free, and I am transformed by the blood of Jesus. I thank You for keeping me and never leaving me. I thank You for Your Son Jesus, who died so that I may live, and for that, God, I am forever grateful. Father, I surrender my life to you, and I will forever give you the glory and honor in Jesus' name, I pray. Amen.

Now that you have surrendered all to God, I want you to take time out just for you and God. I want you to sit down with your journal and write down what you sense God is saying to you. Yes, God talks to you, but most of the time, you are too busy to hear what God is saying. God is always talking. I want you to sit quietly, no TV, no music, no cell phone, just you, God, and a pen and paper.

Now that God has allowed me to give you 17 good, meat-eating chapters, I want you to take your time and digest everything that was written. Write down everything that is required of you, and as you go through each Chapter, write everything that convicted you, impacted, and transformed you throughout this journey. This is not the end of the journey. God has mandated me to do live classes on these same topics over six months to a year.

I thank God for you taking this journey with me, and I pray something God said will transform your life forever.

Love you all to life,

Hope

References

Emotions. (2023). *Oxford English Dictionary (provided by Google)*. Retrieved

August 4, 2023 from https://languages.oup.com/research/oxford-english-dictionary/

Fear. (2023). *Oxford English Dictionary (provided by Google)*. Retrieved

August 4, 2023 from https://languages.oup.com/research/oxford-english-dictionary/

Mind. (2023). *Oxford English Dictionary (provided by Google)*. Retrieved

August 4, 2023 from https://languages.oup.com/research/oxford-english-dictionary/

Psychosis. (2023). *Oxford English Dictionary (provided by Google)*. Retrieved

August 4, 2023 from https://languages.oup.com/research/oxford-english-dictionary/

Soul Ties. (2023). *Oxford English Dictionary (provided by Google)*. Retrieved

August 4, 2023 from https://languages.oup.com/research/oxford-english-dictionary/